SPIRIT REFLECTIONS

by
Olga Mayze

CON-PSY PUBLICATIONS MIDDLESEX

First Edition

© Olga Mayze
2000

Published by

CON-PSY PUBLICATIONS

P.O. BOX 14,
GREENFORD,
MIDDLESEX, UB6 0UF.

ISBN 1 898680 20 5

INDEX

PREFACE

These words were given to me years ago, during a meditation.

I never considered myself a medium and yet with the knowledge that I have Gained over the years, I now realise that God can speak to all humanity if they will but still their minds at times.

We are all part of god you see. We are in truth spirits, here and now. We are each one a spark given off from the great holy spirit, we call God.

Spirit were true to their promise to send someone along to help me get this book into print.

My most grateful thanks to Bunty Streffield for her efforts to help me fulfil the job that Spirit had requested.

TEACHING THROUGH TRANCE

The word of god can never be a printed book,

God is, and his word is like himself an ever present,

Ever living moving power.

What is written can never be more than an historical record

Of what was the word of God to Moses, Samuel, David, Isis or Paul.

The seasons, the flowers, the harvests and the sunshine were

Given ages ago, conclusively.

God continually renews each in its own appointed time.

So it is with his word.

It is like a well of water, bubbling up,

Not a stagnant pool, that for two thousand has maintained

A dead unvarying level.

Men have to learn that he speaks today, if they will but listen,

As much as he ever did.

A printed book only traces the course of the stream in the past.

It cannot show the broadening revelation of the present

by Olga Mayze

Chapter 1
SPIRIT REFLECTIONS

This book is being written at the request of spirit. People who have no awareness of what they are, or psychic happenings so far in their lives, may wonder how spirit can make such a request, this I do believe is to help these people.

I first came to this awareness when I was about 15 years old, I began to wonder where my thoughts were coming from, most of you must have had the same thoughts, when perhaps you or your friends both had the same thoughts, you both started saying the same thing or you had an idea that came to you both at the same time.

You see 69 years later (I am now 84 years old) and after so many psychic things have happened to me in my life time (as I will tell you later in my writings) I now am a dedicated Spiritualist, this does not mean I know everything, but I have been convinced over the years that there is no death, you just cannot die even if you wanted.

We are spirits, each one of us, in physical bodies, here and now and spirit is indestructible. There is no beginning and there is no end to life. We are born into this earthly world to experience all sorts of problems, good and bad so that our spirit selves may develop and progress. Without problems to overcome, how could we have the satisfaction of progressing spiritually. Without suffering how could we learn understanding of what our fellow spirits in the body are suffering. We need to learn compassion for all creatures on this earthly journey. This is why it necessary for us to enter into a physical body, we could not survive in the earth's atmosphere, when we come from the spirit world without this body of flesh.

If you think of an astronaut preparing to walk on the moon, he has to don a space suit to exist in the outer space atmosphere. So we need the physical body to contain the spirit. I once asked one of our spirit teachers where the spirit world is, if you imagine a peach, said the teacher, the earth is the stone in the fruit and the flesh is the spirit regions. There are different levels in the spirit regions and depending how you have lived your life while on the earth plain previously, will decide which level you will ascend or descend to at the end of your term on earth.

Normal decent people need have no fear, when the time comes to go back home to the spirit world, if we were perfect we would not have come to earth. The spirit teachers say there is great rejoicing when a spirit being returns back home, in other words, when our physical bodies of flesh get to the stage of being unable to hold or sustain our spirit bodies, either because of old age, illness or accident. If someone commits suicide they often bitterly regret it, because they still find themselves with the same problems they were trying to escape from, in other words, they had failed in one of the tasks or lessons, that they had, perhaps, been born into a body to live on Earth to learn. Even if we fail in our tasks or lessons if we try or make an effort, that is enough.

We must always remember we have our Guardian Angels and other good spirits always trying to help us in anyway they can. If someone commits suicide through illness or brain damage or disease they are able to progress with no hindrance, they are not responsible. Our loved ones who have passed before us and spirit helpers who have tried to guide and support us through our earthly lives, are there to welcome us home, the spirit teachers tell us we are reborn into the spirit regions and there is great rejoicing as we on earth rejoice at a new life being born into the family. Think of the rejoicing and congratulations on awakening from so called death.

When we come to the earthly regions we know which lessons we need to learn, even if we are not consciously aware of that, it is imbedded in our spirit selves. This is why it is helpful if we can be aware of our higher selves, and always remembering that we are like receiving sets, transmitting thoughts and also receiving them, therefore, if we are endeavouring to progress spiritually, we must remember, that, if we send out bad thoughts to other people, we are harming ourselves more, than those we are directing them to. We must learn tolerance and try always to see the good side of other people, send out thoughts of healing to people whom you meet and you believe need healing. Ask spirit to try and help people who have sunk so low in life's conditions, and never refuse to help anyone, even if it is just a kind word of encouragement, you are obeying your higher self. Try to achieve a balance in your character and thinking. Try to understand others' problems. You will find your life will go smoothly, not without problems, remember we are here to learn lessons.

As we interact with other people, situations are presented to us to enable us to progress, it is our free will that we take advantage of these situations if we want to stretch ourselves spiritually. Some people, overlooking the plight of people struggling through life, to whom they could perhaps give a little help, but are too busy in their efforts to accumulate much wealth and worldly goods, may imagine they are living life to the full, not thinking that they cannot take their wealth with them. When this earthly life ends, which it surely will, some of the people who have struggled in their earthly life, but always tried to help others, will find they have progressed when they have returned to spirit, where money has no meaning and the rich people of earthly life, find they are no richer spiritually than when they were last born into an earthly body, they have wasted their time on earth and failed to learn the tasks they came to earth to learn, ignoring the opportunities that were presented to them, each soul is responsible for their own progress. As the old saying goes, God helps those who help themselves.

When we see or hear of people acting cruelly to other people, some ignorant people will say, "Why does God allow things like this to happen? God gave us free-will otherwise how could we progress and make our own way to the higher realms. Why does God let these people get away with their evil deeds, people ask. Just remember this time on earth has a limit to it. It is not the end, but a new beginning. When we return to our own loved ones, then the evil doer's find they were not so clever as they believed. They will go to the lower regions of spirit, where they have earned the right to mix with people of their level, perhaps worse than themselves and dwell in the regions of darkness. If they wish to repent there are spirit people who are willing to help them. It may take centuries before they can make amends though for their evil deeds, and come into the light once more.

These people living on the lowest vibration, are close to earth's vibration and still with evil intentions, can sometimes latch on to drug users or alcoholics and encourage them to continue in their bad habits. They themselves cannot continue with their own vices once they have left the body, so they get pleasure from encouraging other weak souls still in the physical body to continue with their obsession by influencing their minds.

So this is why people are told not to try contacting the spirit world for amusement, by treating it as a game with a glass or plantchet or other means, you may attract these low mischievous spirits.

Always go to a spiritual church or a trained developed medium if you wish to develop your own spiritual gifts. It tells you in the Bible {Corinthians} we all have gifts of the spirit. Some have the gift of seeing {clairvoyance} some the gift of hearing (clairaudience), some are clairsensient. Neither seeing or hearing but sensing some have the gift of healing and some the gift of giving love and comforting others, the peace makers.

The gifts are stronger in some than in others, but it takes time and commitment to develop our gifts. You will need to sit in a development class with a good medium. We are told, a good medium is born, no amount of trying to choose what you would like to be will help, if the gift is not there, but rest assured there is always something, some gift that you are blessed with.

I had been running our local church with the help of two or three devoted helpers. I once went home feeling tired and thinking I had no special gifts, why? I asked spirit, I have been a believer all these years, why can't I stand on the platform and give out messages of comfort to those who come seeking. In my depression I picked up a book lying at my side, I opened it at random, and as my eyes fell on the print, I started to read, "one of the most important tasks in the spiritual movement is in running a church, without a place to come for learning where would the people go, how would they get their knowledge". I thanked spirit for that lesson.

Even washing the cups and saucers after services and the cleaning of the centre, is spirit work, and just as important. Spirit is with you and rejoicing that you are helping to carry the truth to people who are seeking knowledge.

As you go seeking a medium, always remember that even with this wonderful gift all mediums are on a different level, some are more developed than others, in other words, do not be gullible, test the spirit world, and even though they maybe good mediums, trust your own judgement. Sometimes, a medium can misinterpret what they are getting, they may see a symbol and not quite understand what they are getting for you.

Another saying from the Bible "seek and you will find" mediums are like a telephone instrument, they link you with your spirit loved ones. Some people have said, "if our loved ones are still alive, why don't I get a message from them" Well these people will never go to a spiritual centre, so if they have not developed their own gifts, how can their loved ones contact them without a medium, (A spiritual telephone instrument.) You cannot speak to a relative in the next town if you do not have a telephone to link you. Even if you don't get a message from someone you have lost when you go to a spiritual centre, you will get pleasure hearing other people's messages and realise that if their loved ones can contact them it will eventually be your turn to get proof that those you thought had lost for ever are still close to you and are caring about you and are aware of what you have been doing. Believe me, we have lots of laughter in our meetings as people are linked with those they thought they would never hear from again.

They are the same personalities as they were on earth. Your mind is the spirit part of you, your brain is the physical, it is like a computer. So your loved ones takes all the memories with them, they are the same personalities.

The spirit is indestructible, that is the real part of all of us, so we must start taking more notice of our own thoughts and try to make time to sit quietly, to calm our minds, perhaps with a little soothing restful music, as Harry Edward's, the great Spiritual Healer once said, "if a window becomes steamed up how can you see through it?" Sometimes spirit will manage to register on our computer brain, we are going somewhere and suddenly decide not to go to that particular place, then later we find we have perhaps escaped some nasty situation through changing our minds.

People have decided at the last moment not to fly on a particular aeroplane later to discover that the plane has crashed, all passengers were killed.

We may sense danger somewhere and decide to go a different way, but for the "Grace of God" we say, I may have been involved in that incident. We are told that we are never alone.

Each baby born onto this earth is given a Guardian Angel to guide it through life. This spirit or angel can be a member of your family who has previously passed into spirit, my own guardian angel is my great Great grandmother, she died years before I was born, but I have had so much proof from different mediums with descriptions of her , I have a psychic portrait of her, I have photos of her that cannot be denied.

Sometimes in a church service mediums will say to a person, "I have your Grandmother or Grandfather here", and the people will shake their heads and say oh! I do not know anything about my Grandparents. They forget that their Grandparents may have passed to the spirit world years before they were born, but they still are aware of you and have been keeping a loving watch on you from the spirit world even if you never feel you knew them. You are still a part of their family. So perhaps they will want to guide and help you through your earthly life. There will be a link of love, that cannot be broken.

I often think though, it must be very frustrating for our own guides and helpers in the spirit world when they are trying to help us and the only way they can get through to us is by impressing our minds and our thoughts, so we really should be trying to become aware more of thoughts that pop into our minds. Sometimes at odd times, when we are standing at the sink washing pots, our minds are idling, I remember once, (this was when we were living in Spalding) I was ironing at 9 pm, I was alone, and we had no telephone in those days. My father was in hospital in Derby, I lived in Lincolnshire, we had visited my father the day before and he was getting along nicely after his bowel operation, so I was quite easy about his condition. I was watching a film on television as I ironed, but suddenly got an urge to phone through to the Derby infirmary to ask how my father was. It felt so urgent I pulled the plug on my iron, grabbed my bicycle and rushed up the road to the phone box. The nurse said, I am so glad you have phoned, your father has to have another operation, we could not contact your mother in Derby (no phone again) will you let your mother know please.

We were able to go early next morning, pick up my mother and get to hospital. Fortunately Dad recovered and they later came to live with us in Lincolnshire. I could have told myself Dad's all right stop worrying, but spirit got through to me as I am sure they try to do to ease life for us while

10

on this earth we dwell. Please do not get the idea you must walk around listening to your thoughts all day and people perhaps saying that person is always day dreaming. Remember you have come on this earth plane to learn lessons, you are a spirit in a physical body, you must try to achieve a balance. Even though you realise you are a spirit you still have to live out your physical life, we are earthly people, we are not perfect, or we would be in the higher realms with spirit, just go along the way you feel impressed, try to control bad thoughts, it is difficult at times as we all know (they may come back on you) and remember if you hit a bad patch in your life this may be a lesson you are here to learn from this bad experience, try to overcome feelings of despair at your present situations, ask spirit to give you strength to overcome your problems, and accept that you are in a situation that you will learn a lesson from, and so emerge a stronger and more understanding spirit.

Remember, that iron-ore needs to go through a fiery furnace before it emerges as steel, be strong and always remember you are not alone.

We are told by spirit teachers there are seven levels on the spirit plains, when we pass to the spirit side we go to the level we have earned through our lives on earth, it is impossible for us to go to a higher level than we have earned or progressed to, Higher Spirits and teachers are able to transform themselves down to our lower level regions to teach and talk to us.

People who do not understand say, Why are a lot of our teachers Indians, Chinese or of Eastern races?. The Indians were a very spiritual race when on earth, they lived very close to nature. That was before the white people destroyed their way of life.

The Chinese have always worshiped their ancestors who had passed to the higher life, their civilisations are so much older than ours but they are wonderful teachers, and some are sacrificing their own progression to transform to our lower regions so that they may help us understand what life is all about. It is said that Jesus is one of the teachers, these teachers do not give the names they used when on earth, they assume names from nature. They do not wish to be worshiped, they just wish to serve. Silver Birch is one great teacher, Golden Eagle and many more united in one aim to help humankind.

I have been privileged to see one of my teachers, I was in the bath when he passed before my sight, an Indian with one feather at the back of his head, I was given the name White Cloud, I quickly jumped out of the bath and did a quick charcoal sketch of him, it must be about 16 years ago now. About 7 years ago a medium said to me as I was passing her, "did you know that you have a red Indian guide, Olga", "oh yes," I replied, "I get the name of Silver Cloud," she said. That was good enough for me, I said, "o.k. I thought it was White Cloud."

People often laugh and shudder when I say I saw him whilst in the bath, but you must remember that water is a conductor of electricity, and this is why these things are made possible, the conditions are just right. I used to have visions when I went into the bathroom first thing in the morning, I liked to splash my face with cold water, and as I did, I often used to have visions of an Indian camp, and an Indian girl, I must have had a previous life as an Indian in the past. As children we were taught that "God" was a benign old person with a flowing beard.

After being in the movement for over 67 years, this is my idea now of God.

If there are seven levels of spirit I believe that God is the collection of spirits that have reached the level of pure spirit the highest vibration on the seventh or top level over the centuries. There is certainly a governing body over the earth plain. These spirits must have lived countless earthly lives in all conditions and are now one wholeness of refined spirit.

We are all free to hold our own idea of God. When we were created we were all given free-will. People say, "when I was in trouble God came to me and helped me," yes, the spirit of God helped you, because the spirit of God is in all things, all creatures, but when we stop to think about it, God needs the tools or instruments to help him in his work and we people in the body, must be forever sending out an SOS as we go through our earthly lives.

I sincerely believe that when we ask for help, it is often our loved ones who have passed into the spirit world, before us, who help us, they are the instruments of 'God', as we all are while still in the body. God is in each one of us.

We are told that as a sparrow falls to the ground, God knows about it. That was illustrated to me a few years ago. We had a lovely alsation dog whom I used to take for long lonely walks along a river side in Lincolnshire, the banks of the river were built high for flood protection along which we walked. The river on one side of the path, then a steep bank down to the levels of the fields, a little dyke between the field and the river bank that went on for miles, with no interruption. I never met a living soul.

The dog trotting in front of me, just enjoying the peace and quiet and space, when suddenly I had a tremendous urge to go down the bank on the field side, down I went and stopped at the side of the dyke and gazed into this little narrow drainage stream. Right in front of me in the water was a little stoat threshing about, I thought, oh how lovely it is playing in the water, but as I watched, it suddenly died, it was in its death throes, which I had mistaken for play. It stretched its little body out and was gone to an animal spirit world. I thanked the spirit for showing me that little animal, and asked a blessing on its little soul, as I continued my walk I realised the truth of the saying that God knows when a little creature dies. One of Gods helpers had managed to demonstrate that truth to me because I was relaxed and calm and at peace with the world. So it is when we are asleep, spirit are able sometimes to contact our higher selves to help us.

Chapter 2
THE WAR YEARS

During the war years, I realised the souls in the spirit realms were very active trying to help us people on earth who were suffering very hard times.

My son was born in 1945 my husband still away in the army, my 6 year old daughter in one bedroom and my baby next to my bed in his cot. My son's breathing was very bad, I felt so worried, so I prayed to spirit, asking for healing for him, I dozed off and after a while I became aware of a beautiful vision at the bottom of his cot it seemed to cover the wall facing us, life sized. There appeared a lovely red glow, as I watched, I saw a group of people dressed in biblical clothes gazing down at a baby in a crib, they just stood looking at the baby which was a vision of Jesus in the manger, as I watched the vision gradually faded into the wall, I fell asleep again and next morning my baby son was fit and well.

That bedroom in the middle of Derby must have been a very psychic room I had two more visions there. I woke another night from a deep sleep to see a big white light in the corner near my window, like a full moon, it had rays shining from the lower part of it, as I looked at it, it moved right across the opposite wall, I panicked I thought it was a search light shining in my room and my blackout curtain had come down, older people will remember, we all had to have blackout curtains or shutters up at the windows, a warden would have been after us if we showed any light, enemy planes could have bombed us in an industrial town. I jumped out of bed but my curtains were closed tight, I thanked spirit for letting me know they were watching over me.

My third vision in that room was sad. I had a cellar in that house and just a grating in the street where the coal was shunted down. I woke from a deep sleep to see a soldier at the foot of my bed, I can still see that vision as though it was yesterday. My first thoughts when I saw the soldier was, that someone had got in through the cellar grating. Then my second thought, as I looked, I realised it was a vision, oh, something has happened to Harold (my husband) this vision was so clear and in colour. The soldier was dressed just in his shirt, sleeves rolled up, shirt neck opened lighter neck band than the khaki shirt, lighter coloured braces on his high waisted khaki trousers, he was crouched down and as I watched all fear seemed to leave me, the soldier dived from the foot of my bed, and into my dressing table, the vision disappeared. I seemed to doze off, next I became aware of a monk walking past my bed, his head was down, I could not see his face but he just disappeared into the wall at the back of my bed, it was a terraced house.

A short while later my next door neighbour received a telegram to say that her son Harry had been killed in a bomb raid abroad in Italy. I must have seen Harry diving for cover into a trench when the bombing started. I asked spirit why I had been shown that, as I know that there is always a reason for something.

After an interval I told my neighbour what I had seen and asked her to go to the Spiritualist church with me, which she did, and eventually she joined a development circle and Harry used to come through to her.

As you can imagine she gained great comfort from that. She was older than me at that time, so I do believe they have been re-united now in Higher Realms.

Unlike some of the orthodox religions, we Spiritualists believe that Jesus was the worlds greatest healer and medium. He was a great spirit, come to earth in an ordinary physical body to heal and to help us. We do believe he is one of the greatest spiritual teachers still working and giving encouragement.

I sat in circle with friends in the 1970s I had a vision of Jesus, holding up a lamp, the light of the world". I was stunned and thought no one would believe me, so I kept it to myself, I did not tell a soul. A few weeks later my friend said to me, what do you think, a lady told me that last week she had seen Jesus, how ridiculous. Why, I said, Jesus is still working in the spirit world. He worked amongst the ordinary people whilst he was on earth, why should he not still be working amongst the ordinary people now. I thought, thank goodness I had not said that I had also seen him, for I would not have been believed either.

Weeks later in a public service at Stansted Hall, the Sanctuary was packed, the medium said I am coming to the person against the window, pointing to me, she said, you have seen Jesus. Yes", I said. I knew I had seen him (no doubts then) spirit had proved it to me.

1970s again, I was alone meditating I must have gone into a light trance, I gazed at a large as life vision of a Jewish Rabbi on a plain wall in our lounge. He had a lovely face with a white beard in profile, he was of a big build with his scull cap on his white hair. The whole vision was in sepia colours and lasted quite a few seconds. The funny thing is I have been given lots of guides and helpers from mediums over the years, but never a Jewish Rabbi, pondering over it one day recently, it occurred to me that I had given my daughter a Jewish name.

When she was born my husband and I discussed names but had not decided one definitely. Soon after she was born the nurse came to my bedside with a form to fill in. What name have you given your daughter, she said. Without stopping to think, I said, Judith". There must be a link somewhere in a past life.

15

Chapter 3
VISIONS

When we were still living in Derby after the war 1945, my husband was de-mobbed and resumed his studies to further his career in local government. He was successful in passing his final exams, in the meantime I was still attending the services at the Spiritualist churches in Derby.

My husband, now having letters after his name, had started applying for jobs in different towns, I received a message at church saying, "You are wanting to move?" Yes that's right, I said. You will move in the new year", she said. Trouble was, she did not say which new year.

New year came around and I got ready, cleaned the house ready to move. Next new year cleaned again but no move. Four years went by, I was beginning to doubt spirit by this time, the medium was wrong. Harold had been short listed at Rochester in Kent, he had his interview and returned by train the next day, New Year's eve.

I sat knitting and listening to the wireless as I waited for him to come home. It was the Scottish New Year celebrations programme on the radio. The announcer said, In one minute, Big Ben will chime bringing in the New Year 1949. Just at that moment I heard Harold's key turn in the front door, he walked into the room, just as Big Ben chimed, he said, You can start packing now I got the job.

So do not ever give up if spirit tells you something will happen, you see, there is no time on the other side, so they can miscalculate.

Connected to that move, months before, I began having vivid psychic dreams, spirit were showing me the places where I was going to move to.

The first was Rochester Station, I had never been further south than a day trip to London from Derby in all my life, but in my dream I saw a wide yellow river (tidal) with a paved esplanade and strong railings running along side of it and the ruins of a Castle on the left of me. I saw that later, as I came out of the station at Rochester, the river Medway.

My second vision about that time was about another station again. In my vision, we got off the train and walked off the platform and through the booking hall, as we came outside, I was surprised to see the railway lines and rail wagons, they were banana trucks of which I had no knowledge.

Then I finally came to live in Spalding I found that the wagons belonged to Geest's. They had their own separate railway lines outside the station. It was a unique sight, sadly to say, they are gone now, due I think to modernisation of the area.

I was shown another place in a dream that I was to move to in the future. That was in Essex, I found myself walking down a road leading to a cul-de-sac, as the houses finished I walked down a footpath leading to open fields. We found a house we liked there when we left Spalding, just a few yards from the end of the cul-de-sac.

I was also aware of a clear dream of another place I was to move to in the future, when I was walking down a road (quite a rural place) I was walking down this rough road and looked up at the people passing me going in the opposite direction, but they were behind a hedge on a higher level than me.

This is where I live now, the higher level that I saw the people walking on is a playing field at the bottom of where I live only a few yards away.

So now I am convinced that our lives are planned, and we should go along with our feelings that feel right to us. Yes, we have free-will, but I feel that if we go against these feelings either through fear of the future or other reasons, then often our lives go wrong and we start to have problems.

Not everybody is destined to move about the country as we did, do not feel you have to move just for the sake of moving.

Chapter 4
STORY OF THE HALLS OF LEARNING.

Another psychic dream about that time, spirit took me to see the halls of learning in the spirit realms. Once we go back to spirit we can continue to learn anything we wish. All the great scholars and teachers who have ever been on earth before are there to teach those who wish to continue their progression.

I found myself walking through a magnificent hall there were other people strolling about, as we walked I gazed at some beautiful large double doors, they were magnificently carved and one door was open halfway. As I looked into the hall I could see rows of women standing and looking towards what I presumed was a platform, but I could not see that.

The women were all dressed alike either as nurses or nuns. As I walked further I saw another large double door, also beautifully carved, this door though was short about $1/3$ of the height of the other, later I asked a medium what that one was for as it was closed tight. The medium's interpretation of that was. When you go through that door, you go on your knees to meet God.

About that time I had another clear psychic dream. I was back at the halls of learning, there were people moving about again, but I was standing in front of a desk, a lady was writing, she suddenly looked up and saw me, Are you still here, she said. With that I awoke in my bed, I believe some of us, if we wish, go into the spirit world to work during sleep time.

I thought we had settled down to prepare for retirement, w hen we moved to a new house in Spalding. In those days I could travel to London from Spalding for £1.50 return (a day return on the train) a friend and I liked to go to the SAGB. The Spiritualist Association of Great Britain, Belgrave Square. (It is still there.)

We would go for a private reading, lectures and services and get a good meal in the basement. We would spend a good day with the spirits. My Harold would say, "I won't fill my football coupon in till you get back with the winning numbers. Well! Have you got the winning numbers for me," he said, this particular time "no" I said, "the medium says we are going to move", "do not talk silly" Says he, or words to that effect. "Do you think we are going to move after all the work we have done on the new house." "Well," says I, "that's what I said to the medium, I told her we had just moved and were getting ready for our retirement. She shook her head, the wheels are beginning to turn, my dear, you are going to move further south, you won't have so far to come here then, you have big trees near to you now," she said, I replied, "yes that is right well there are a lot of trees

18

where you will move to, I was told."

From that time on Harold started getting spirit messages, when ever we went to a service, it was always the same message almost word for word, no matter, which church we went to or which unknown (to us) medium, the message was, There is a job for you to do for spirit" the mediums seemed to get a bit mixed up describing the job that had to done. Spirit were showing them big financial ledgers and surveyors' tapes. To us that represented local government jobs. Then the mediums seemed to get confused. It all became clear later. We still could not accept that we would move again. No way!.

As the medium said, the wheels were beginning to turn. I still see her winding her hands round and round each other as she told me.

Local government was being re-organised, all the existing councils were being gathered into large district councils, so the local councils were finished. My Harold took early retirement, he was offered the Chief Financial Officers job but turned it down, he was 58 then.

We thought we could be happy using our touring caravan, but before winter was over Harold was bored and was needing a purpose to his life. The big district councils advert created jobs to keep the local people in touch. These were town clerks', but they were only more or less part time jobs, so I suggested that Harold might get one of those jobs and I was willing to move again.

Forgetting what spirit had said, he started applying for jobs up north, he got on short lists, but, either did not fancy them or was not offered the job. I said to him, you have been told by spirit the job you get is further south.

He applied for a job at Epping, but the application date was over, so he phoned Epping and asked the secretary if the job had been filled, she said no, no-one had been appointed, but if we would like to go to Epping the next Saturday she would get the Council in to interview him. He got the job right away. So we moved to Essex, as easy as that.

That was where the spirit symbols came in, the accounts ledgers.... Surveyors tapes. You see sprit had us moved and we settled in, the trees were where we went through Epping forest to get to our house that we had bought.

We were very content, it was lovely and we were only a few miles from Arthur Findlay's home, Stansted Hall, which had been given to the Spiritualists for a college for physic studies. That became our local Spiritualists' Church after a while though, the Spiritualists' National Union needed a general secretary. This was the real job that spirit wanted Harold for.

This was why they had got us moved to Essex, also Harold was

19

becoming bored with the council job there was not enough for him to do. The Epping council were sorry to lose him but understood his need to work for the Spiritualists. The money from the council had helped us become established for spirit - they had organised us very well. Ready to take on the General Secretary's job, so much for our not wanting to leave our new house at Spalding.

I do not think anyone would argue that Harold did a good job at Stansted, he put the office into good working order, he was Chair of the building fund pool. The assets had for the first time exceeded one million pounds and the general reserve stood at over one hundred thousand pounds. He was also a member of the Trust Property Committee, he did a lot of work in helping churches who were in trust with the Union, helping them to get grants, interest free loans and advances to help them in times of difficulty with their buildings. He eventually became Chairman of the Trust Property Committee.

He worked with the Union for three years, but his health was failing, I could see the strain was telling on him, so not wanting to lose him, I persuaded him to retire, he had done the job spirit had asked of him, but even then we discovered there was another job waiting to be taken on. We agreed to move back to Lincolnshire again, I wanted him to relax. We decided to go back to Spalding again, little did we know we were being manipulated by spirit again.

We could not find a property in Spalding that we wanted, we were getting old and needed one with a small garden and near to the shops and a bungalow. On our second trip from Essex to Lincolnshire, we were beginning to think we would never find the place we wanted. We stopped in Bourne for lunch and a review of the agents leaflets. Look", I said, we had this leaflet last time we came and we have never looked at this one, Right, said Harold, as soon as we have had lunch I'll go in the agents and get the key to view.

When we found the property in Coggles Causeway, we walked in looked around, looked at each other and this is it.

The property had stood empty for 18 months, the seller had priced it too high. Harold made an offer and it was accepted, it had been waiting for us.

Before we left Epping I was at Epping church, the medium said to me, "You are thinking of moving my dear," "Yes, next week", I said. She then said that "you have five years hard work in front of you," I replied, "Thank you very much," you see spirit had lined up another job for us.

There had been a lady running a spiritual meeting in Bourne, (a room in the old court house), but she had to finish just before we left

Spalding to go to Essex, so Bourne was without a meeting place in the meantime, 2 months earlier, a group of people had started another one, a few weeks before we moved back to Bourne, in a very poor building, but in the centre of the town, after a few weeks, I think it had proved to be a bigger task than they thought.

The new president approached Harold and asked if he would take it over from them. "I am sorry, we have come here to retire," he said. We were now 68 years old, Harold's health was failing. "Oh, Please take it over," said Mr Cormey, "I can't keep it going, it is going to shut again if you don't do it, nobody else will take it on." "Perhaps we could just keep it ticking over, by just having the one service on the Saturday evening," I said. (It had always been on a Saturday in Bourne) "until someone comes along to take over." Harold allowed me to persuade him, so we took on another task.

Sadly Harold died just five years later, yes, it had been five hard years work, the Epping medium had passed the message on correctly. I carried on the task with a few good friends until I reached 80, then spirit found a new willing worker to take over the Bourne spiritual centre. We are now going from strength to strength.

The Epping medium did not tell me that I had eight years hard work after Harold had passed to the higher life. I was given the strength to do the job though and I know that Harold was with me all the way. I was not alone, none of us are. We are all instruments of spirit, how could they get the job done on the earth without the tools.

All this evidence proves though that our lives are planned ahead of us. Future events are already in existence.

Three years ago, I once more had a trip to the Spiritualist Association of Great Britain (SAGB).

I was fortunate to book Glyn Edward's as my medium. I had never met him before, he hadn't a clue where I had come from, but, he asked me if I could take the town Bourne, (where I live now), he told me I had something to do with a church. "Yes", I said. Amongst a lot of other information, he said, Is your husbands name up in that church. "No", I replied. He clasped his head, he knew and trusted his guides and helpers, they could not be wrong, but, I still insisted Harold's name was not up in the church, which it was not. Twelve months later when I was 80 someone was kind enough to take over the job of running the centre. I was given a good retirement send off, I was presented with flowers and as I took them I noticed a lace cover on the podium, I did think, whatever have they put that there for, it looks a bit odd. I returned to my seat and looked towards the platform. I suddenly jumped up again and went back to the front of the gathering, there was a lovely plaque on the front of the podium.

With loving thanks to Harold (deceased) and Olga for keeping this church open, I had not told anyone about my message, but 12 months later Glyn Edward's was right, Harold's name was in the church. Spirit knew 12 months previously.

There is no time in the spirit world as we know it, time is man made. Time for rest! I thought that we had finished with our tasks when I retired from the centre, but no. I had a two year rest, but then I started getting spirit messages again, different mediums, all unknown to me, but they all passed the same message, all the regular Spiritualists to our church started laughing with me each time I got the message. Spirit people realise you are getting older, but there is one more task to be done. I used to sink into my chair, what else could I do? I was already doing reflexology to help the animal welfare funds and healing. I was soon given a clue.

I visited an old friend who had lived in Bourne all his life, he is the same age 82. One day when I called he was busy writing, "What on earth are you writing Henry," I asked. "I am writing about my life in Bourne," he replied. He was a country person, lived on a farm all his life. "What a nice idea," I said.

On the way home I thought I could write down about some of the psychic happenings that I have experienced in my life. So I started jotting down some of the happenings. The next Saturday evening service, (a stranger to me) medium said that spirit wanted me to start writing. I laughed, then said that I had already started this last week. Good, said the medium, spirit want you to write a book. What me! I said, I can't even type Oh, someone will come along with computer knowledge to help you. She replied.

At last I had been told what my next job was. I had to do it for spirit. I was in a daze. I could not do anything like that. Oh! We of little faith. What is the point of living if we do not do anything to help spread a little knowledge. We are well rewarded for anything we did for spirit.

While at the Arthur Findlay College we were privileged to attend a Gordon Higginson materialisation seance. A never to be forgotten sight.

Gordon retired to a curtained off cabinet, after first going out of the room with two volunteer members of the congregation to examine Gordon, just to make sure, he was not hiding anything about his person that he could fake the phenomenal sight we were about to see. There was only a plain wooden chair in the cabinet. The room was packed, the atmosphere was electric, not a sound was heard. Then we started hearing voices, a child's voice, Gordons little coloured spirit girl helper called Cuckoo and a mans voice, Gordons' guide. They were speaking with each other.

As we all sat watching the cabinet, just a small red light was showing, we saw a cloud of ectoplasm, (like white vapour), coming from the bottom of the cabinet, it seemed to bubble out until it built up in front of the cabinet and gradually formed the shape of a human, still it appeared to be draped in white, it moved forward and spoke to a lady on the front row, I cannot be certain but I believe it was her father. He said, Why is your sister sitting at the back of the room, the sister's voice came from the back, there was a bit of personal chat between them then the spirit held out his hand for two or three people to touch. They said it felt quite warm and solid. After awhile the figure seemed to shrink and gradually disappeared, we could hear the spirit helpers speaking again in the cabinet, it sounded quite a normal exchange of instructions to each other as we listened. The curtains were drawn back to reveal Gordon still sitting in the chair still in a trance.

We were privileged again to attend another materialisation seance by Gordon. This time though, before we were allowed to enter the room, all the people there were asked to leave all tape recorders and cameras or any other thing of metal, such as large watches outside the seance room because it was dangerous for Gordon.

As before the room was packed, Gordon went out to be searched by two men. He was only wearing thin trousers and a sleeveless vest. We could hear the spirit controls speaking again from the small curtained cabinet. (A voice box is built from ectoplasm). Then I saw a crinoline lady of ectoplasm pass behind the cabinet, I could hardly believe what I had seen, but it was reported in the next weeks psychic press, others had seen her, so I had to believe.

Sadly though soon after the lady had disappeared we heard voices again coming from the cabinet, it seemed that something was wrong. Gordon was ill. Some stupid person had disobeyed the instruction not to take any metal object into the seance room. Poor Gordon Higginson had suffered radiation burns to his solar plexus. He had to be helped to his bed and was quite ill for a long time.

Chapter 5
GORDON HIGGINSON

Gordon was a natural medium, his mother was a well-known medium before him, he had other brothers and a sister I believe, but Gordon was the only one with the gift from his mother.

There are many instances with little children up to the age of 5 to 6 years when they appeared to be playing with another child, (invisible to us). The parents put it down to imagination or tell the child to stop being silly, but it must be remembered the child has not long since come from the spirit world, and would remember. In some cases the memories fade after a few years. Mediums in later years have said that their parents told them not to be silly when they have said that they could see spirit, then the gift has been suppressed, and the child has kept quiet about what they have seen, yet that person has a natural gift for mediumship.

Gordon used to tell us the story of when he was a small child, he used to play ball with a spirit child, he would throw the ball across the room and the ball would come bouncing back to him. This unnerved his father who was looking after the children while his wife was out taking a church service. When the father went to the pub one night he told his friends about this son of his, his friends laughed and said, oh! Go on, we do not believe you. So he invited his friends home to see for themselves.

As Gordon got older his dad told his mum to take Gordon with her, with the result that Gordon was on the platform by the time he was 11 years old. One night when he was working, someone threw a brick through the church window, (some people were against and afraid of Spiritualism in those days), but Gordons' mother was sitting in the front row while Gordon was on platform, he said she told him to carry on and ignore the brick. A lot of people were afraid to go to a meeting.

I remember going to one in 1940, I was surprised to see one of my neighbours there. We came out to-together, up a passage to the road, I was going to step right out, but she was terrified, and she grabbed me and pulled me back, then she carefully poked her head round the passage and looked both ways to see if the coast was clear, then I got the signal to proceed, (what a giggle).

Chapter 6
PHILIPPINE PSYCHIC HEALERS

We were in the college when the Philippines' psychic healers came to England, Helen and David Alisaldys. We were there on the Sunday when the Committee and friends were introduced to them, they had arrived the day before, more or less with just the things they stood up in, no case or portmanteau, I tell you this because they were accused of faking and using pigs blood when they performed their operations.

They were banned from coming to England again. It was a miscarriage of justice though I had worked in a hospital for ten years, so I volunteered with another lady to help them as they did the operations. We had hundreds of people over the weeks coming, all nationalities, we worked continually from 9.00 a.m. till about 5.00 p.m. For weeks.

I was watching in one of the cubicles all the time. There was blood, I was given the swabs to dump in a dustbin sack, there was no attempt to hide it, I don't know where the officials who condemned them thought they got all the pigs blood from, they came as strangers to our country, as I said, no luggage, it was hot weather at the time so where could they have stored the blood, they had no fridge in the rooms they were given to live in, they certainly could not have arranged with a British butcher to supply them.

When they started the operations they both wore skimpy summer clothes. There was no place they could have concealed it. When we were introduced to them on the Sunday before the sessions started the next day (Monday) we were all chatting about their work, Harold said, "You want to have a go on that one", pointing to me. My thoughts to my husband at that moment were anything but spiritual. "Why, what is wrong," asked David. "Oh, I suffer badly from cramp in both my legs, they seize up the length of my legs, Harold has to massage them regularly," I replied. Before I knew what was happening I was on the bed with my stomach bared to all the visitors gathered around to witness the psychic operation. I had pulled my clothes up and skirt and knickers down to expose my abdomen but forgotten to pull my petticoat up from underneath me. I heard David say to Helen, "the menstrual area," "yes" said Helen as she performed the operation. She appeared to knead my abdomen, I felt no pain, but I did become aware of a brilliant blue flash and then it was all over. I had no cuts just a slight red mark and my petticoat was all stained with blood. (my cramps stopped) I have slight cramps in my feet now but I was clear for about 20 years) I smelt the blood on my skirt when I got home and it certainly did not smell like pigs blood.

Helen was an Anglo Indian, she had been married to a doctor, but he released her from their marriage to do her spirit work. In the Philippines she married David and they used to send any money they made back to the Philippines to help David's family, brothers and sisters who were living in poverty. I am sure they will be still doing good work somewhere in the world.

David had treated a lady who had come to have deafness cured, he let her walk the length of the sanctuary, as she got to the far end David said in a very soft voice, "Can you hear me lady?" She whipped round, "Yes," she had heard him, we all laughed in happiness for her.

About that time I was being used as an instrument for healing, my guide was a Scottish doctor, I was given a psychic portrait of him by Coral Polge, one day in the 1970's in London SAGB. (he has a lovely face), I was also given a portrait of a Sister of Mercy, Sister Agnes, at the same sitting. I knew a bit about her but somehow I did not like the drawing I had of Sister Agnes, I just did not feel it was right.

About 3 years later I had a private sitting with Ursula Robert's, another famous medium working at the Arthur Findlay college. "You are working as a healer?" She said "yes, that's right" I replied. "There is a Scottish doctor here who tells me that he works through you, and you have a portrait of him, he's very pleased with the picture, it is a very good likeness, but spirit was not pleased with the portrait of the Sister of Mercy, they hadn't got the eyes right." Can you imagine my amazement at this proof being given after three years.

We had some very good healing over the years, but the quickest one we had amazed me and the patient's family too. The wife of the patient, an elderly man in his seventies, asked for healing for her husband in the Essex hospital. I met her and her grown up son in the car park, as we walked to the wards she told me her husband had been ill for quite a few weeks, and had gradually lost consciousness.

Previously the doctor's had said squeeze my hand if you can hear me and he did, but, he had stopped responding even to that now. He had his bed moved to the position near to the door when we entered the ward. He was deeply unconscious and did not acknowledge his visitors at all. I placed my hands on his chest and forehead, and to everyone's amazement after a few seconds, he stated coughing and then he opened his eyes, looked at me and said, "Who are you?" His wife said, "this lady is a healer darling, she has come to try and help you," "oh! and where do you come from," he asked, "Takely village," I replied, "Oh, I used to keep my cows in a field there." (He was a farmer), he was quite rationale by this time, his other son had arrived at his bedside and all they could say was, "it's fantastic". I thought so too, I had never seen such a quick reaction.

He wanted to go home right away but the doctors understandably could not agree to that and managed to keep him in the hospital for another week, he was out in the fields working on his tractor with-in a few weeks, and lived quite a few years actively after that, passing into his eighties, his wife and family are still my friends I still tell them it was spirit doctors that did the healing, I was only an instrument.

I had been passing the healing energies to Bill a man suffering from cancer, he had been kept reasonably free from pain. I went to his home on a Friday morning as usual and said I would see him after the week-end, we were going away for the week-end. That night in the caravan, I had a psychic dream. (Psychic dreams are very clear and they do not fade as normal dream tends to do.)

In my dream, I was walking up a grassy hill as I reached the top I came face to face with a man walking along the top. Hello Bill, I said, what are you doing here?. I'm looking for mother he said, as he spoke, I glanced down the other side of the hill, there was a cluster of houses, and two ladies coming up the field at the back of the houses. Oh, here she comes", he said.

When we reached home on Sunday evening I found a note on the mat from Bill's wife.

"Dear Olga, just to let you know on Friday after you left, Bill, said, oh Thelma, I feel so tired, So I got our son to help him to bed, he just lay down and went to sleep. He died in his sleep."

I told Thelma I had seen him looking for his mother and I saw her coming to meet him. That would be my mother, he thought the world of her, she said.

Some people get the wrong idea of spirit healing, it is always to help the patient, but sometimes it is to give help and relief from pain and stress until it is time for a person to pass to a higher life, we are told there is a time for us to be born and a time for us to die, and often the gift of spiritual healing is used to help souls pass peacefully. You will notice I do not say Faith healing as some people think of it. All healing comes from spirit. Faith does not come into it. Babies are healed as are animals, they cannot have faith. Mothers give healing when they comfort their child, after a fall or when anyone sends out a thought for healing, when they see anyone or an animal in pain or distress, as I said before our thoughts are living things they go out into the ether and are heard by some loving Spirit.

To find out if you can be a channel for spiritual healing try to calm your mind and reach out into the ether, ask that you may be used as a channel for spirit healing. Lift up your mind and clear it of earthly thought, lightly lay your hands on the person or animal to be healed and just tune in to spirit for a

27

few moments, or just direct your own thoughts to where the pain is.

You can direct your healing thoughts to any pain you may have yourself, after a while you will feel heat around that area. It is a matter of tuning your thoughts into spirit channels and keeping your own thoughts always on a high level, always seeing the best in everyone, there is always a best side.

You need to attract good spirits to use you, remember we are surrounded by spirit but as people were on earth, so they will be in spirit regions, they are not all good spirits, they perhaps have not developed to the higher vibrations. Ask for protection from your own Guardian Angel, if you feel at all threatened, raise your thoughts to Higher Realms, and ask God to help those low spirits to progress.

Through giving out love and trying to help others this is how we all progress spiritually, that is the reason for our earthly life.

Chapter 7
ANIMALS CHAPTER

My father passed to spirit thirty years ago, but fifteen years later he proved to me he was still near me. He was a great animal lover he always carried a trick photo of a white terrier dog in his wallet, the dog was curled up asleep in the photo, but when people looked at it, it looked like an ugly face or a pitted potato when it was turned upside down on the photo.

In those days there was no television or radio, remember things like that were a talking point to get conversation going. One morning, I was half awake when I was surprised to have a vision of a white terrier dogs face all in golden light. The face came right up to mine, it's nose almost touching mine. I was suddenly wide awake, where has that come from. I thought, I have never had one look like that.

I could have understood if it had been a vision of one of my pets that had gone to the spirit world. Our pets still live on after so called death. Two days later, I went to post a letter, passing by a paper shop in the village, I walked right passed the shop to the corner of the road, then I stopped. I thought I will just go back and read the notices on the glass door of the shop and look at the for sales. Lost and found adverts, I had been going to that shop for ages and never glanced at the notices before. Right at eye level, the first notice that I looked at said, found wandering and almost dead from starvation, small white terrier dog, now needs loving home, phone riding stables.

I already had two cats, but I thought that my daughter might like it. She had a dog and had once said that it would be nice to have another to keep it company while they were at work. So I phoned the riding stables to see if they still had the little dog. Yes, they had.

Thinking of my vision, I asked. "What does it look like?" "Well, it's got a terrier body, I don't know quite how to describe it's head," she said. "Is it a bit like a whippets face," I asked. "Exactly," she replied. There was a silence on the phone then I thought, if I say I had seen it in a vision, she might think, oh! We have got a queer one here. So I said that we would be along later.

My son-in-law said, "no, they didn't want another dog, one was enough for them." So I said to Harold, "I saw that little terrier dog the other morning in a vision," "Well, lets go and get it then," he said. We found the riding stables, it seemed that they had two pedigree dogs running around and one of them had found the lost dog curled up in some hay an a barn almost dead. He was a bag of bones, that is why his little face looked like a whippet.

They were going to put him to sleep if no one wanted him or claimed him. We were the only people to enquire. We said that we would have him, but could not take him home then in case someone came to claim him. He would have to wait until the following Wednesday, when the week was up (by law) it seemed that we were the only enquiry they had had about him.

The lady phoned me the next week, on the Tuesday, December the second, she asked if I still wanted the little dog. "Oh yes, someone at church has given me a log casket for his bed, he has got all his blankets and bedding in it all ready," I told her. "Right," she said, "I am going to bring him to you this morning" (a day early).

It was the anniversary of my father's birthday December 2nd when Charlie arrived. We had decided to call him Charlie after Harrolds guide, a cockney barrow boy. The lady carried him in, he had a scrap of old pink flannelette blanket tied on with string, we took his coat off, and he just laid down on the carpet, our Siamese Burmese cross cat came over to him, he just laid still and Squirrel Puss walked all round him sniffing at each of his feet in turn, he never flinched, she took to him straight away, she new he was ill, they became the best of friends and travelled miles to-together in the car, exchanging beds with each other on the back seat. They went everywhere with us.

Sushi the other Siamese cat we had was a bit nasty and used to strike out at the other two if they went near her. She had, had a bad life, until we took her in, she was old and had spent her life on a bed with a man who was bed-ridden, she could hardly walk when we first had her.

Harold used to carry her to the top of a big lawn we had, put her down and walk away. She gradually got that she could run back to the house, her legs and tail going in all directions as she ran, but she loved it and would run straight into the kitchen and up the stairs and give a yowl of delight. We were able to give her three years of love, before she died.

We called our other cat Squirrel, because when she was a kitten she used to fluff her tail out like a squirrel, silly name for a cat really, but wonderful proof later from spirit.

Charlie survived Squirrel Puss by three years, he was a great comfort to me when Harold passed suddenly. I used to take Charlie to church with me when I cleaned the church on Saturday mornings, he was quite happy wandering about as I worked.

Three mediums over the years since I lost him (3 years ago) have said to me that I have a small white dog here on platform. "Oh yes" I said, "he was used to coming here".

A few weeks ago a medium said, "I've got a Siamese cat up here

30

on the platform!". "I believe it's mine," I said. "Wait a moment," said Sue the medium, "I will see if I can get a name for you," she tuned into spirit for a second, then I saw her face drop. "I'm sorry" she said "I can't get a name but I will tell you what I'm being shown. All they are showing me is a Squirrel". "Well, that is the cat's name," I said. Everybody in church laughed. That was wonderful evidence, who would have thought of calling a cat Squirrel. Then I thought, the pair of them are following me to church now, Charlie is bringing his friend.

So you who have lost a beloved pet, do not grieve too much, know that they are still close to you, you will see them again.

I had further proof that my pets are still in the house. A few weeks after Charlie had gone, the house felt so empty, I was dusting when I heard a voice say, You could give a home to an old cat. Within a few minutes I was on the phone to the cats home asking if they had an old cat that nobody wanted. The lady said, Yes, would you like to come and see him, I went right away. He looked like Felix, I realised spirit had been working on me for a few weeks previously, I had been taking great pleasure in watching the adverts for Felix Cat Food. What a lovely cat I used to think.

My Thomas was old and had been shut in a small shed at the bottom of the orchard, the lady looking after him was killing him with kindness, too much dried food and no exercise, he hardly had any room to exercise, I put his first meal down for him and he could not bend to get to the dish, he had to lie on the floor on his tummy to reach the food, spread eagled, legs stretched out. I asked what is his name and was told spike, well that's no name, so I called him Thomas. I do not think he had ever known any love, he was terrified of men, at first, if he heard a man's voice he would run to hide. He's a lovely old can now, he is still a bit tubby but he has his freedom and never stays away too long. Thomas adopted next doors kitten, Daisy, when she arrived last year, they love each other now, sometimes, he will hold her down and give her a good licking all over, he always leaves her a bit of dinner when she comes in on her daily visits, even though she has plenty of food at home.

I must tell you though how psychic pets are though, the first night for Thomas in his new home, I put a blanket on the top of my bed and invited him to sleep there with me, he accepted the invitation and sat on the blanket first of all washing his face and looking very relaxed and contented, he suddenly glanced up at the wall behind the bed, he stopped licking his paws and he froze, his eyes nearly popping out of his head, he stared for a second then he bounded off the bed.

I realised my other pets had resented his presence and had frightened him off. I gave them a good telling off and told them to leave him alone, he needed a home and love. I believe they have accepted him now, he is quite relaxed now and at home, but very rarely settles on my bed and I sometimes see him staring at something or someone just as Squirrel used to.

A few years ago, we had an alsation dog, we were hosts to a medium. I said that I must take the dog for a short walk before we go to the church, I would love to come with you, she said. We started off to go over the fields, she started laughing, Oh, how I wish you could see this, we have a crowd of spirit dogs coming with us, all trotting happily along with us, she said. "What a wonderful gift clairvoyance is".

When we are forced through illness or accident to have our pets put to sleep or when they pass over naturally, they, being spirit beings the same as humans and often with a strong spirit link of love to humans and happy memories, when the vet releases them the dear pets spirit, their instinct would naturally be to cling to you, (follow you home if away at the vet) Back to the place where they were loved, and wait patiently for the time when you will be reunited.

There are many animal lovers in the spirit realms who devote their time to caring for our animal friends, just send out thoughts of love to them and they will be waiting to welcome us when our time comes to go home to the higher realms.

My husband had a queer sense of humour and through that he gave me irrefutable evidence that he was still with me and had come on this walk with us. Anyone who is a bit queasy, please pass over the next few lines.

I was on holiday with my family and we were out walking on a nature trail in Wales. Four of us and my dog, Charlie, were all going at our own pace, quite a distance from each other. The dog busy smelling all the country smells, and we were at the end and I was waiting for him. As dogs will do, he did his daily duty. As a loving owner, I glanced at him to see his health was normal, but it was not, I suspected he had passed worms. No one about, the family all way out in front, I stooped to take a closer look, telling myself that I must get a worm tablet when I returned home. We continued the walk not a word was said.

That evening my friends, Lily and David, who live in Wales, they came to pick me up, we were going out for an evening meal, we had not met for years. Lily is a medium, we sat waiting with a drink for our meal to be served, suddenly Lily started laughing, David and I asked what was she laughing at. Oh, Harold!, She said between giggles, what is he saying we asked. She replied, He was with you to-day on your walk, did you bend down to see what Charlie had done? What evidence, how could I doubt he was not with me.

It must be difficult for a loved one to find something unusual to prove they are with us, think about it. We are so inclined to doubt so many incidents which could apply to anyone.

Two weeks after Harold's funeral, my kitchen clock stopped, I thought the battery had gone and so I would go out to-morrow and get another. In the meantime, I put a small bedroom clock on top of the TV in a corner of the kitchen, it goes for 24hours and I needed a clock in the kitchen.

Next day I bought a battery and put it in the wall clock, no go, Oh, well, I thought, we have had the clock 20 years. The next day I went out and bought another one, put it up on the wall but that one wouldn't go, so back I went to Woolworth's It won't go", I said, "Well, it won't, he replied, you have put the battery in the wrong way. Back home I go again and got it going, in the meantime, I had not given the little bedroom clock another thought. Three days later, my next door neighbour came round to see if I was all right, "Yes, I'm ok" I said. "Have you had a man in the house this morning, I can smell his smoke, was he smoking a pipe?" She asked. "No. Nobody has smoked in the house since Harold had passed two weeks ago," I replied. "Well it smelt just like Harold's tobacco," said Greta. I made us a cup of coffee and we sat at the table in the kitchen, Greta noticed the new clock on the wall. "Oh, I like your new clock, has it got a tick?" She asked. We both listened intently, not a sound. We continued with our coffee, a few seconds later, we looked at each other in surprise and both looked at the wall clock, there was a noisy ticking sound, it was not the wall clock but the small bedroom clock ticking merrily away in the corner on the top of the TV, it continued ticking for a quarter of an hour, Greta slightly naturally psychic, but very nervous said, "What does that mean."

"It is Harold letting us know that he is here with us, it was his pipe tobacco you smelt when you came in," I told her. I had forgotten to wind the small clock again, it must have run down 2 days previously. Sadly for me, my friend Greta has since joined Harold in the spirit world, her family have smelt perfume in their home since she left.

One circle we held in Essex, six people sat. Harold always put a brand new tape in the machine every week, we watched him take it from the cellophane, load it into the machine and switch on just before we started with a prayer.

At the end of the sitting we played it back. We did that for a few weeks. One week we were rewarded. It was my turn to open in prayer, just before my prayer there was music on the tape, it was old fashioned string instrument music, (chamber music). It started playing, then my voice was heard, music continuing to play as I gave the opening prayer. Our Siamese cat decided there was too much power in the room she cried to be let out.

The music still playing, the sound of me getting up to open the door to let her out, the music continued for a few seconds then finished. There was no sound in the room apart from the cat and the door creaking just on the tape.

Our friends asked if they could borrow the tape to make a copy of it and then they found music on both sides of the tape, after they had made their copy.

Chapter 8
PARK SEAT

A circle I have sat in, in recent years since Harold went to the higher life, had a lady who was endeavouring to develop as a psychic artist, she used to draw a lady's face each week, the same face. We were in a darkened room and I could hear her pencil scribbling away. "What have you drawn this week Marie," I asked, when we had put the light on. "Oh, it's just the same face again," she replied. Despondently, holding it up. "Oh no it's not," I said, "look there is some printing on the top of the face," in pencil was an attempt by my Harold to write his name. He improved on it the following week, it said "Olga, I am all right, love Harold x" the following week I fell and fractured my wrist, it was Easter week, next circle night Harold wrote again, "please be more careful Olga, I love you, x". It was getting clearer each week.

Sadly though Marie was going through a traumatic time in her life and our circle came to an end, but what treasures I do possess. Proof again that our loved ones are near us, another occasion I had wonderful proof.

A few weeks before Harold passed in 1988, we were both out in the park walking Charlie, it was the year of our Golden Wedding. Harold said, I have had an idea, I would like to have a park seat put here to commemorate our Golden Wedding in August. That's a nice idea", I said. Sadly Harold passed on the 4th February, the celebration was not to be.

A few weeks after the funeral, I thought, I will put a seat in the park in memory of Harold. I made the arrangements and the gardener phoned one day and said, Mrs Mayze the seat has arrived, if you put on your wellingtons one morning you can show me where you want the seat putting".

Next morning Charlie and I went to the park, I stopped dead in my tracks, I suddenly realised I was singing out loud, what was I doing, I had nothing to sing about, I had felt more like crying and trying to control my emotions. Then I realised what I was singing, "Take my hand, I'm a stranger in paradise." That was a song Harold would have sung, I was never into sentimental songs. Oh bless him, he was with me.

Sadly I have had to have the seat moved now, because of vandals it is not in the place Harold wanted it, it is still in the park though facing the road. Proof once again that spirit are always near us.

For years I have had great faith in Biochemic tissue salts, they are minerals of 12 different kinds almost a different one for nearly all our ailments. I had a book for reference of which number to take. These books are very hard to obtain. One day looking through my ageing book, I had it for years, I thought, what shall I do when this book gets too old to read.

I thought no more of it then, but about a week later, imagine my surprise when the postman handed me a parcel. I opened it to find a new Biochemical tissue salt book and two boxes of tissue salts, one for asthma and one for colds and flu. There was nothing else in the parcel, no bill, no invoice.

That weekend I was host to a medium (Graham Nisbitt) when he arrived he was suffering badly from asthma, also one of my friends went down with a bad attack of flu. I keep most tissue salts in the house but these were combinations of the minerals that I did not have. My friends said that I would get an invoice from them later, I never have though, another odd thing, if the book had come from a publisher they would not sell tissue salts or vica-versa.

The oddest thing was though that there was a little gold label on the back of the book, with an address in Wellingborough. Oh good I thought, I will send for another book, to that address. I posted my request and a cheque to the address, about three weeks later the post office returned my cheque and letter with address unknown stamped all over it. I never did get an invoice. I thanked spirit.

When Harold first started taking services he told me, he always saw a blue cross, so I said, we must look around and see if we can find you an earthly one. So started the hunt for a blue cross. For months we searched, if we saw something in blue, I would say is this the blue you see, always the reply would be no, that's not it.

One day out shopping in Chelmsford we wandered into a large department store. I was still determined to find a blue cross, I went straight to the jewellry display, it was full of modern reasonably cheap jewellry, most, gold coloured, but then I spied a blue cross on a dull metal background in the middle of all the gold coloured pieces, it looked like an antique, the blue stone cross on top of the metal cross had small flecks of gold in it. I quickly went in search of Harold, Come and look at this, is this the colour you see?, I said. "Yes, it is", he answered. How much is the blue cross, I asked the assistant, she lifted it out of the display, there was no price on it, but she said that she would go and enquire. To my surprise it was quite a reasonable price, I had been prepared to pay much more for it, we were convinced it was second hand, but why was it amongst all the modern jewellry. It became a very treasured possession. On the back stamped into the metal was the trade name Miracle.

If we have achieved any progress at all with our spirit selves as I believe most of us do, on our return to our spirit homes, if we have suffered a long and exhausting illness or a sudden and violent passing, we would be

36

taken to a spiritual rest home so that the spirit may have time to recover the trauma of so called death.

These homes are in beautiful surroundings among flowers and trees and loving spirits to care for us.

After a while each soul is taken to a private place and left alone, there they will be able to see (like a video) a record of the life they has just recently lived in earth conditions. There is no one to judge us, that is left to our own consciousness, we are able to see the mistakes we made or the success, and progress spiritually. It is said that everything in our lives is recorded.

If I have helped only one or two people to understand what life is all about I am happy to have achieved that.

I have found great peace and contentment in my old years just knowing my loved ones and members of my parents families whom I have never got to meet are still about and knowing I will meet some of them when my great day comes and I shall leave this earthly plane and join dear Ones who have gone before me.

I shall be worrying about my children I have left behind then and thinking why can't I get through to them and help them in their troubles. They have their own lessons to learn though. We are each responsible for ourselves. *May we never forget God is within each one of us.*

Olga Mayze

THE END.